*T*O

*F*ROM

OTHER HELEN EXLEY GIFTBOOKS

For a super friend
For a wonderful grandchild
For a lovely mother
My Daughter, my joy...

For Jen, Gemma, Dana, Carolyn and Amy —
daughters that any parent would be proud of.

Printed simultaneously in 2002 by Helen Exley Giftbooks in Great Britain
and by Helen Exley Giftbooks LLC in the USA.
12 11 10 9 8 7 6 5

Illustrated by Juliette Clarke. Written by Siân E. Morgan.
Edited and words selected by Helen Exley. Printed in China.

Helen Exley Giftbooks, 16 Chalk Hill, Watford, Herts WD19 4BG, UK.
Helen Exley Giftbooks LLC, 185 Main Street, Spencer, MA 01562, USA.
www.helenexleygiftbooks.com

Helen Exley Giftbooks cover the most powerful of all human
relationships: love between couples, the bonds within families and
between friends. No expense is spared in making sure that each book
is as thoughtful and meaningful a gift as it is possible to create:
good to give, good to receive. You have the result in your hands.
If you have loved it — tell others! There is no power on earth like
the word-of-mouth recommendation of friends.

A HELEN EXLEY GIFTBOOK

For a beautiful daughter

Written by Siân E. Morgan
Illustrated by Juliette Clarke

⧲EXLEY

I love all your hellos

I love to see you bounding up the path, full of all your news.
With a crumpled picture from your bag and a story about what's happened, told with such speed I think you're going to run out of breath.

Or a tale of how your date went — you chatter excitedly, editing certain bits for my benefit!

Ever since you first came into my life there always seems to be some exciting news.
And each day with you seems to bring anticipation and excitement, something more to discover.

I never know what the day will bring.
That's the beauty of having a daughter.

I LOVE ALL THOSE HELLOS,
ONES THAT START WITH A GREAT BIG HUG OR A
QUICK TOUCH ON MY HAND.
IN FACT, ANY SORT OF HUG WILL DO.

A lifetime of smiles

WE HAVE FILLED THE HOUSE
WITH A LIFETIME OF LAUGHTER
CRAMMED WITH SO MANY
MEMORIES.

I love your smiles, I see them everywhere.
No matter where I am, no matter where you are,
your smiles will always stay with me.

How could I forget them – that baby smile,
looking right at me as I fetch you from your cot,
that toddler smile as you burst into the bedroom
to make sure I'm awake and ready for action,
the smile after your first date or the smile when
you get your first job. And not forgetting that
smile after you've been naughty!

Even if you're not here, those memories of you
dance around me, wherever I go.

A lifetime of memories

I LOVE ALL THOSE KEEPSAKES THAT
HAVE ACCUMULATED OVER THE YEARS.
EACH ONE TELLS A DIFFERENT STORY.

Your first baby shoes, books with teeth marks and scribbles, toys that have had the life loved out of them, your first tooth, locks of hair.

There are notches in the door frame that marked your growth. And scars and scratches on the walls that signal minor disasters or wild games.

I remember you creeping into my bed in the middle of the night because you were scared or lonely in your own room.

You took over completely and wriggled about as I perched on a sliver of bed – without any covers! Then I would listen carefully as you breathed deeper and deeper, slowly falling fast asleep; warm, comfortable and safe.

Watching you grow

I love to look at all those photos of you. How they make me laugh when I rediscover them again. No hair, baby hair, bright red hair! No clothes, baby gros, dressing-up clothes, clothes that make me hold my breath!

I remember so clearly those things you did for the very first time.... Watching you go to school, with me feeling proud, anxious and nervous, all at once! ... Your first play when I sat in the audience and whispered your lines along with you.

I love being there, in the front row, watching your every move with anticipation and love.
I will try my very best to be there whenever I can, as long as I possibly can be.

I LOVE ALL THE DIFFERENT YOUS...
THE CUTE FLUFFY-HAIRED BABY,
THE ADORABLE WICKED LITTLE GIRL,
THE DEVELOPING TEENAGE GIRL,
(WITH A MIND OF HER OWN!),
THE ACCOMPLISHED YOUNG WOMAN.

Gifts! Surprises!

DAUGHTERS GIVE SUCH THOUGHTFUL
GIFTS. ONES THAT TAKE TIME AND
EFFORT, ONES THAT ARE INGENIOUS,
SIMPLE ONES, EXTRAVAGANT ONES,
IN FACT ALL HER GIFTS ARE WELCOME!

*Homemade surprises that everyone else knows
about weeks in advance are a daughter speciality.
Even if they use up most of the kitchen supplies!*

*And then there are fine delicate ornaments sent
halfway around the world – and miraculously
managing to arrive in one piece.*

What surprises daughters give.
Daisy chain necklaces that come down to the
knees, breakfast in bed and paintings and
drawings galore to adorn the fridge and every
available wall space!

I remember those sweets you saved all day for
me that were covered in fluff! And your first cake
(even if you did eat most of the mixture before
you baked it!).

Your gifts could be dinosaurs made of old
cardboard tubes or my special perfume or gems.
I have loved them all the same, because they
were from you.

I love you – warts and all

A daughter can slam doors, break vases, take clothes without asking, stay out late and not call, paint the TV when you can't afford a new one, and try to drill the back door. All outrageous deeds are forgiven.

Daughters have their own opinions. They make you think about yours as well. Sometimes it's good; it helps to get your ideas out and give them an airing so you re-examine what you think.

Sometimes I stand there, telling you off for something that I am guilty of myself (which you are usually very quick to point out).
Only a daughter could point out my flaws and get away with it!

No one else could be so easily
forgiven for dropping everything
across chairs, beds and floors.
No one but you.

... feeling like my heart is being wrenched.

Missing you

I have always dreaded our goodbyes.
Ever since I first watched your tiny frame
standing in the doorway, waving bye-bye with
that little hand of yours as I left. Desperately
wishing I was the one who was staying with you
all day and feeling guilty that I wasn't.

And those goodbyes as I left for longer and you
kept asking me if I was coming back, just to
reassure yourself.

Or those goodbyes on the phone as I check that
you are all right, feeling like a part of me is
missing. Feeling like I'm missing out on you,
feeling like my heart is being wrenched if you
cry or need me.

Watching in wonder

I love the expression on your face when you see something magical, something new to you.

Watching a daughter wonder at the beauty of a crimson sunset, a snail crawling across a path, snowflakes, bright stars, or birds feeding on the nuts left outside, is absolutely priceless.

A daughter gives you a great excuse to relive your childhood again!

Even if I've been to a place a hundred times before, it feels different when I go there with you. Almost like I've never been before, almost like I see it through your eyes, with more excitement, anticipation than before.

So often you put your
hand in mine or we link arms and
step out in the world together, just
spellbound in amazement.

Wounds of love

I love your honesty, the honesty that only a daughter dares use. I could ask you anything and you would look me straight in the eye and tell me.

Even if we don't always see eye to eye, it always works out in the end.
I could never stay cross with you for long.

No, I forget my anger even after not speaking, slamming phones, raging voices, tears and exasperation, after saying things neither of us really meant to say.... Such hurtful things for two people who think the world of each other. Wounds which cut deeply because they came from you, because I try to do my best for you.

We've had some fights,
you and I. The sort that only
we could have and still be friends.
(I like it most when we end up
laughing!)

Just looking at you is enough

I could never resist watching you in the living room or out in the garden, or holding long conversations with yourself, absorbed in your own little world.

I have always loved it when I've seen you happy and contented – the two things I always wish for you.

Sometimes I've loved just catching a glimpse of the back of your head as you've worked as I wonder what you are thinking.

It is so funny to hear you talking to yourself, repeating things that I have said. I'm always amazed at what you pick up!

Maybe I just smile to myself as I watch you as you pretend to be a fairy, an aeroplane, a ballet dancer, a shopkeeper, a doctor or whatever you want to be. Dressing up, dancing around, organizing toys, in a complete world of your own, totally oblivious to the fact that I am sitting in the shadows, fascinated, completely entertained by you.

You care for me...

So many times you've worried about me if I am late or go to the doctor or go away on a trip. It always seems so funny when we swap places and you insist that I ring you or you tell me off for coming in too late!

And I might protest at first, but secretly I'm glad when you insist that I put my feet up whilst I have a strong cup of tea.

When I'm down, I'm always glad when you come and give me a hug. Sometimes, you just sit beside me as we talk or watch TV together. Or you bring me interesting, helpful information.

Sometimes you are so thoughtful.
Only you would struggle with
shopping bags that are far too heavy,
or be so keen to unload the groceries.

*You have been known to put the shopping in
such unusual places, that it can take me a week
to find everything!*

Serious things, long talks

I cherish all our talks.
Hurried ones over breakfast, funny ones as we
walk in the park or play in the garden. And
those long ones as I sit on your bed, as you tell
me what's really worrying you.

And I love all those sentences that start with "I
need your help." I can be useful or I can simply
be there, holding my breath, watching and
waiting as you make decisions for yourself.

So many scary moments have been and gone.
Something upsetting on TV, illnesses, bullying or
broken hearts.
And in those moments, realizing nothing else
mattered, absolutely nothing could compare to
your well-being, your health, your safety.

*In those saddest moments,
I am reminded that you're not
completely invincible. Not just yet.
And secretly I'm glad that sometimes,
just sometimes, you still need me.*

You are all
that I could wish for

*I love all those times when I sit and beam
that you are my daughter.*

*I think of you as my best investment, my best
work, my best achievement, the very best thing
I ever did.*

*You are the one topic of conversation that
I would never tire of. The one that always
captivates and entertains me.*

*I watch as you discover yourself
and what you can do, as you become
what you are truly capable of.*